LIBERIA 2016 HUMAN RIGHTS REPORT

EXECUTIVE SUMMARY

Liberia is a constitutional republic with a bicameral national assembly. In 2011 Ellen Johnson Sirleaf of the Unity Party won a second term in multiparty presidential elections domestic and international observers considered generally free and fair. Civilian authorities generally maintained effective control over the security forces.

The most serious human rights abuses were those linked to deficiencies in the administration of justice, official corruption, and violence against women and children, including rape, domestic violence, and human trafficking.

Other important human rights abuses included police abuse, harassment, and intimidation of detainees and others; arbitrary arrest and detention; press harassment; corruption; female genital mutilation/cutting (FGM/C); racial and ethnic discrimination; discrimination against lesbian, gay, bisexual, transgender, and intersex (LGBTI) persons; mob violence; and child labor.

Impunity remained a serious problem despite intermittent and limited government attempts to investigate and prosecute officials accused of abuses, whether in the security forces or elsewhere in the government. Corruption at all levels of government continued to undermine public trust in state institutions.

Section 1. Respect for the Integrity of the Person, Including Freedom from:

a. Arbitrary Deprivation of Life and other Unlawful or Politically Motivated Killings

There were a few reports the government or its agents committed arbitrary or unlawful killings. For example, on February 27, three officers of the Liberia National Police (LNP) Emergency Response Unit responded to a call from Bright Farms rubber plantation in Mount Barclay, where they fired several shots during a confrontation, one of which hit Stephen Bordor--a Bright Farms resident--in the back of the neck, leading to his eventual death. The three officers were dismissed and charged with manslaughter by the magisterial court. They were released on bail, and their cases were submitted to the Montserrado County court for prosecution. The prosecution dismissed charges in October, and the officers were subsequently reinstated.

b. Disappearance

There were no reports of politically motivated disappearances.

c. Torture and Other Cruel, Inhuman, or Degrading Treatment or Punishment

The constitution prohibits practices such as torture and inhuman treatment. Sections 5.1 and 5.6 of the penal code provide criminal penalties for excessive use of force by law enforcement officers and address permissible uses of force during arrest or in preventing the escape of a prisoner from custody. Nonetheless, police and other security officers allegedly abused, harassed, and intimidated persons in police custody. For example, in October a woman was arrested during an LNP raid, and two LNP officers reportedly stripped and beat her severely. They hit her head repeatedly with a nightstick, kicked her between her legs, and stomped on her shins. In a separate incident, the police inspector general directed an investigation into the Grand Gedah LNP commander for abuses including beatings and other human rights violations by police. The LNP commander was relieved of duty pending the outcome of an investigation that had yet to conclude at year's end.

In 2015 the UN's Office of Internal Oversight Services identified the UN Mission in Liberia (UNMIL) as having a high incidence of alleged sexual exploitation and abuse (SEA). The UN's Conduct and Discipline Unit (CDU) of the Department of Field Support identified 85 cases of alleged SEA in the period 2008-14. Of these, five were reported in 2014. One involving military personnel accused of sexual abuse remained under active consideration by both the United Nations and the troop contributing country (Nigeria), which had primary responsibility to investigate and prosecute--if appropriate--alleged misconduct by its uniformed personnel. There were six cases reported in 2015, with no cases substantiated. During the year only one case was reported, involving military personnel, and was still under investigation by both the troop contributing country (Ghana) and CDU. According to the UNMIL chief of staff and the CDU, both responsible for oversight of disciplinary issues, there continued to be problems with personnel involved in transactional sex and breaches of the nonfraternization rule.

In October, UNMIL issued new standard operating procedures on reporting and investigating allegations of misconduct to combat further SEA cases. UNMIL also worked with the Ministry of Gender and Social Protection to integrate its SEA referral pathway with the ministry's own sexual and gender-based violence pathway, and it undertook a comprehensive training and awareness campaign through its Anti-SEA Champions program involving prominent representatives from both UNMIL and local communities.

According to a 2015 UN assessment on Human Rights issues emanating from harmful traditional practices in Liberia, accusations of witchcraft were common in the country and often had "devastating consequences" for those accused, including "trial by ordeal." Although illegal, in some cases public officials or those acting in an official capacity, including tribal chiefs, initiated trial by ordeal. Authorities often failed to investigate or prosecute cases involving trial by ordeal, in part due to the perceived cultural aspects of the practice, and in part due to lack of resources and capacity. Many viewed trial by ordeal as a means of criminal investigation or "fact finding," and it was sometimes employed to investigate crimes that had no connection with accusations of witchcraft. While the Ministry of Internal Affairs-- a ministry that includes many of the chief traditional practitioners and tribal leaders--worked to get traditional practitioners to conform to the country's formal legal framework, the practice of trial by ordeal remained common.

Trial by ordeal included: forcing the ingestion of poison; hanging the accused from a tree by the arms or feet for extended periods of time; requiring the accused to retrieve an item from a pot of hot oil; heating a metal object until it glows red and then applying it to the accused's skin; beatings; rubbing chili pepper and mud into the accused's bodily orifices (including the vagina); depriving the accused of food and water; requiring the accused to sit in the sun or rain for extended periods; forcing the accused to sit on hot coals; and forcing the accused to ingest food or nonfood substances to induce severe vomiting, diarrhea, and other illnesses.

Prison and Detention Center Conditions

Prison conditions were harsh and at times life threatening due to overcrowding, food shortages, lack of sanitary facilities, and inadequate medical care.

Physical Conditions: Inadequate space, bedding and mosquito netting, food, sanitation, ventilation, cooling, lighting, basic and emergency medical care, and potable water contributed to harsh and sometimes life-threatening conditions in the country's 16 prisons and detention centers. Prison officials misappropriated food and other items intended for inmates. Many prisoners supplemented their meals by purchasing food at the prison or receiving food from visitors. The local press and the nongovernmental organization (NGO) Prison Fellowship Liberia (PFL) reported that prison officials threatened prisoners' lives. The Ministry of Justice's

Bureau of Corrections and Rehabilitation (BCR) reported three prisoner deaths through September 15.

According to the BCR, as of September approximately half of the country's 2,023 prisoners were at the Monrovia Central Prison (MCP). This prison operated at nearly two and one-half times its 375-person capacity; 63 percent were pretrial detainees. As of September 14, the MCP population of 917 individuals included seven women and four male juveniles, and there were approximately 20 women in other prisons. Prisons remained understaffed and prison personnel salaries were irregularly paid.

The BCR had eight vehicles but was often unable to transport prisoners and detainees to court or to a hospital. According to BCR officials, this was due to the breakdown of vehicles or lack of fuel. The LNP staff often used personal vehicles or commercial motor bikes to transport prisoners to or from court.

The Ministry of Justice funded the BCR; it did not have a funding allocation under the national budget. Due to inadequate funding, the BCR lacked funds for the purchase of adequate food, maintenance of prison facilities, fuel, vehicle maintenance, cellular or internet communications, and regular and timely payment of employees.

Medical services were available at most of the prisons but not on a daily or 24-hour basis. The only location where medical staff was available Monday through Friday was at the MCP. Health-care workers visited most other prisons and detention centers one to two times per week.

The Ministry of Health and County Health Teams had primary responsibility for the provision of medicines. The United Nations, International Committee of the Red Cross (ICRC), Carter Center, and PFL continued to provide medical services, medicines, and related training and to improve basic sanitary conditions at the MCP and other facilities where such services and conditions remained inadequate. The supply chain for medicines was weak throughout the country; prison medical staff often did not have access to necessary medicines. NGOs and community groups also provided medicines to treat seizures, skin infections, and mental health conditions. The ministry and county health teams replenished medications to treat malaria and tuberculosis only when stocks were exhausted. Since replenishment sometimes took weeks or months, inmates went without medication for lengthy periods.

There were reports of inadequate treatment for ailing inmates and inmates with disabilities. In March the BCR began identifying individuals with special needs, including those with tuberculosis, through screening provided by the Ministry of Health. While the law provides for compassionate release of prisoners who are ill, such release was uncommon because the government had yet to develop a policy to implement the law. Authorities determined whether to release a prisoner on an ad hoc basis. For example, authorities arbitrarily denied the request for compassionate release of a prisoner in Voinjama with prostate cancer who died a month after he submitted the request.

Authorities held men and women in separate cellblocks at the MCP, but in counties with smaller detention facilities, a single cell was designated for female prisoners, and juveniles were held with adults in the same cells. Except at the MCP, which had a juvenile cellblock, children were held in separate cells within adult cellblocks. Because many minors did not have identity documents, they were sometimes misidentified as adults and held in adult cellblocks. There were also reports of inmates in the juvenile facility reaching age 18 who were not transferred to the adult population. Pretrial detainees were generally held with convicted prisoners.

Conditions for women prisoners were somewhat better than for men; women inmates were less likely to suffer from overcrowding and had more freedom to move within the women's section of facilities.

Administration: During the year, BCR capacity declined in part due to reduced support from the Corrections Advisory Unit (CAU) of UNMIL. The BCR relied heavily on the CAU for correctional officer training, logistical support, and other financial assistance. While the government continued to make efforts to improve recordkeeping on prisoners, the official process was manual and problems remained. Prior to the UNMIL drawdown, the BCR maintained a prison roll that included prisoners from all facilities at headquarters. After the drawdown, the BCR ceased preparation of the complete prison roll, modernization efforts, and the transfer of paper records from field facilities to headquarters. The roll included prisoner names, dates of entry into prison and sentencing, and courts of initial appearance, but it did not include court appearance dates and other relevant information. It was not always accurate.

Testing of an electronic recordkeeping system and a biometric intake processing system ceased. Developed through a cooperative international initiative by two NGOs and a donor country, progress ceased due to inconsistent access to electricity and the internet, lack of computer maintenance, virus attacks, and insufficient government support.

Authorities sometimes used alternatives to prison sentencing for nonviolent offenders, but courts failed to make adequate efforts to employ alternatives to incarceration at the pretrial stages of criminal proceedings. Courts issued probationary sentences in some cases for nonviolent offenders. A supervised pretrial release program has been used in circuit courts in conjunction with the Magistrate Sitting Program to expedite the administration of justice, but it was not widely used outside Monrovia. During the year public defenders introduced a plea-bargaining system in some courts. The law provides for bail, including release on the detainee's own recognizance. The bail system, however, was inefficient and susceptible to corruption. No ombudsman system operated on behalf of prisoners and detainees.

Staff complaints prompted a July investigation of the prison system by the BCR in conjunction with the MOJ Internal Audit Division that revealed corruption in the distribution of food, including misappropriation. In prior years NGOs reported severe food shortages, but Ministry of Justice central administration records showed sufficient food purchased and sent to facility warehouses. In one instance at MCP, prison officials allegedly sold food taken from a BCR warehouse to inmates through a prison canteen. The prison superintendent in that case was dismissed but not charged and prosecuted after investigation.

The government did not make internal reports and investigations into allegations of inhuman conditions in prisons public; however, the BCR sometimes made prison statistics publicly available.

Independent Monitoring: The government permitted independent monitoring of prison conditions by local human rights groups, international NGOs, the United Nations, the ICRC, diplomatic personnel, and media. Some human rights groups, including domestic and international organizations, regularly visited detainees at police headquarters and prisoners in the MCP.

Improvements: The ICRC worked with the BCR to implement a system-wide food chain management and distribution system, including mandatory recordkeeping for any food coming into the prison system. It also performed body mass index checks on all prisoners, every three months at the MCP and every six months at the other 15 facilities in the country. The ICRC provided therapeutic feeding supplements for underweight inmates at the MCP; the majority of them were newly arrived or inmates with pre-existing health problems.

The UNMIL CAU worked with the BCR to improve the latter's accountability and adherence to international corrections standards. In addition to mentoring, advising, and capacity building, the unit assisted with refurbishment and rehabilitation of facilities. For example, UNMIL installed solar lights at 10 facilities and built a new cellblock in Robertsport. UNMIL officers also provided constant access to cellular, computers, and internet services helped increase communications among different prisons.

In late August, UNICEF funded renovation of the juvenile cells at the MCP. The ICRC provided soap to all prison facilities bimonthly, other hygiene items to the MCP, and essential medicines to all 16 prisons and detention centers. The ICRC also worked with the Ministry of Justice to improve water supply in five prisons, water infrastructure improvement in four prisons, and sanitation and waste infrastructure in four facilities. The ICRC also worked to establish a comprehensive prison health-care system and improve food distribution and documentation, renovated kitchens in three prisons, installed energy efficient stoves in four prisons, and did capacity building for prison maintenance teams so that facilities could perform basic repairs in-house. It built an exercise yard for cellblock D at the MCP that prison authorities began using during the year to give prisoners outdoor access for up to one hour a day. With the assistance of international donors, the government hired and trained 137 additional correctional officers during the year.

d. Arbitrary Arrest or Detention

The constitution prohibits arbitrary arrest and detention, but the government did not always observe these prohibitions. The arbitrary arrest, assault, and detention of citizens continued. For example, in May an LNP patrol officer reportedly beat a suspect while in custody, and the detainee later died from his injuries. The officer was suspended for one month. An investigation of the incident concluded that there might have been other causes of the suspect's injuries.

Police officers or magistrates frequently detained citizens for owing money to a complainant. On August 8, Chief Justice Francis Korkpor ordered judges and magistrates to stop issuing criminal writs of arrest without the approval of prosecutors from the Ministry of Justice or based on case-specific police requests. Despite Korkpor's order, some magistrates continued to order writs of arrest in exchange for payment from complainants. This occurred in both civil cases and criminal cases.

Role of the Police and Security Apparatus

Prior to June 30, the government shared security responsibility with UNMIL. The Ministry of Justice has responsibility for enforcing laws and maintaining order through supervision of the LNP and other law enforcement agencies. The armed forces, under the Ministry of National Defense, provide external security but also have some domestic security responsibilities, specifically coastal patrolling by the Liberian Coast Guard.

The Independent National Commission on Human Rights reported that violent police action during arrests was the most common complaint of misconduct. The LNP's Professional Standards Division is responsible for investigating allegations of police misconduct and referring cases for prosecution. There were instances during the year in which civilian security forces acted with impunity. During the year the legislature passed and the president signed a new police act that mandates establishment of a civilian complaints review board to improve accountability and oversight. In January 2015 officers of the division participated in a three-day training activity related to a plan intended to decentralize its operations into five regions; training covered division policy and procedure, investigation, and report writing.

An armed forces disciplinary board investigates alleged misconduct and abuses by military personnel. The armed forces administer nonjudicial punishment. As of September the disciplinary board had no active cases. In accordance with a memorandum of understanding between the ministries of justice and defense, the armed forces refer capital cases to the civil court system for adjudication.

Arrest Procedures and Treatment of Detainees

In general police must have warrants issued by a magistrate to make arrests. The law allows for arrests without a warrant if necessary paperwork is filed immediately afterwards for review by the appropriate authority. Arrests often were made without judicial authorization, and warrants were sometimes issued without sufficient evidence.

The law provides that authorities either charge or release detainees within 48 hours, and detainees generally were informed of the charges against them upon arrest and sometimes brought before a judge for arraignment within 48 hours. Once jailed, those arraigned were often held in lengthy pretrial detention. Some detainees, particularly among the majority who lacked the means to hire a lawyer, were held for more than 48 hours without charge. The law also provides that, once detained, a criminal defendant must be indicted during the next succeeding term of court after arrest or, if the indicted defendant is not tried within the next succeeding court term and no cause is given, the case against the defendant is to be dismissed; nevertheless, cases were rarely dismissed on either ground.

The law provides for bail for all noncapital or drug-related criminal offenses; it severely limits bail for individuals charged with capital offenses or serious sexual crimes. Detainees have the right to prompt access to counsel, visits from family members, and, if indigent, an attorney provided by the state in criminal cases. The government frequently did not respect these rights, and indigent defendants appearing in magistrate courts--the venue in which most cases are initiated--were rarely provided state-funded counsel. Public defender offices remained understaffed and underfunded, and some allegedly charged indigent clients for their services. Although official policy allows suspects detained to communicate with others, including a lawyer or family member, inadequate provision of telephone services resulted in many inmates being unable to communicate with anyone outside of the detention facility. House arrest was rarely used.

Arbitrary Arrest: Security forces continued to make arbitrary arrests, especially during major holidays, in an effort reportedly to prevent expected criminal activity. For example, on October 3, the LNP launched "Operation Visibility," aimed at demonstrating police presence to counteract violent crime in high-crime communities. This resulted in the arrest of drug dealers and users on the assumption of a high probability of committing a crime, rather than in response to actual evidence of criminal activity. During the operation the LNP also cleared streets and raided suspected criminal hideouts and other sites to prevent the return of petty criminals.

Pretrial Detention: Although the law provides for a defendant to receive an expeditious trial, lengthy pretrial and prearraignment detention remained serious problems. As of September 14, an estimated 63 percent of prisoners were pretrial detainees despite the large number of detainees released by the Magistrate Sitting Program during 2015. Nevertheless, this was a decline from 78 percent the previous year. Unavailability of counsel at the early stages of proceedings contributed to prolonged pretrial detention. A 2013 study of the MCP population revealed pretrial detainees were held on average more than 10 months. On

September 22, the Ministry of Justice installed a public defender at the MCP, in an effort to increase pretrial detainee case processing.

The corrections system continued to develop its capacity to implement probation, including the use of the supervised pretrial release program. In some cases, however, the length of pretrial detention exceeded the maximum length of sentence that could be imposed for the alleged crime. A shortage of trained prosecutors and public defenders, poor court administration and file management, inadequate police investigation and evidence collection, and judicial corruption exacerbated the incidence and duration of pretrial detention.

Detainee's Ability to Challenge Lawfulness of Detention before a Court: Persons arrested or detained, regardless of whether on criminal or other grounds, are entitled to challenge in court the legal basis or arbitrary nature of their detention and to obtain prompt release. The government frequently did not respect these rights, and the court system lacked the capacity to process promptly most cases. Additionally, public defenders lacked the capacity to file the requisite motions, and many clients lacked the means to hire private attorneys to do so.

e. Denial of Fair Public Trial

The constitution provides for an independent judiciary, but judges and magistrates were subject to influence and engaged in corruption. Uneven application of the law and unequal distribution of personnel and resources remained problems throughout the judicial system. The government continued efforts to harmonize the formal and traditional customary justice systems, in particular through campaigns to encourage trial of criminal cases in formal courts. Traditional leaders were encouraged to defer to police investigators and prosecutors in cases involving murder, rape, and human trafficking, as well as some civil cases that could be resolved in either formal or traditional systems.

Trial Procedures

By law trials are public. Circuit court but not magistrate court proceedings may be by jury. In some cases defendants may select a bench trial. Jurors were subject to influence and corrupt practices that undermined their neutrality. Defendants have the right to be present at their trials, consult with an attorney in a timely manner, and have access to government-held evidence relevant to their case. Defendants have the right to be informed of charges promptly and in detail. If a defendant, complainant, or witness does not speak or understand English, the court provides interpreters for the trial. Interpreters are not provided throughout the legal process, however. For example, there are no accommodations or sign-language interpreters provided for the deaf, and rarely is free interpretation available, unless paid for by the defendant. Defendants also have the right to a trial without delay and to have adequate time and facilities to prepare their defense, although these rights often were not observed. Defendants are presumed innocent, and they have the right to confront and question prosecution or plaintiff witnesses, present their own evidence and witnesses, and appeal adverse decisions. The law extends the above rights to all defendants. These rights, however, were not observed and were rarely enforced.

Established to expedite the trials of persons detained at the MCP, the Magistrate Sitting Program suffered from poor coordination among judges, prosecutors, defense counsels, and corrections personnel; deficient docket management; inappropriate involvement of extrajudicial actors; and lack of logistical support. Some local NGOs continued to provide legal services to indigent defendants and others who had no representation. The Liberian National Bar Association continued to offer limited pro bono legal services to the indigent. Financial constraints remained a major challenge in recruiting experienced lawyers for this service. Many lawyers also could not practice because they failed to pay bar association dues, further limiting the pool from which the association could draw pro bono attorneys. Ranging from L$20,000 ($223) to L$30,000 ($335) per year, bar dues are very expensive when compared to the World Bank's 2015 estimated per capita gross national income of L$38,000 ($424) for the country.

According to PFL, women had less access to the courts and on average spent significantly longer periods in pretrial detention.

Political Prisoners and Detainees

There were no reports of political prisoners or detainees.

Civil Judicial Procedures and Remedies

No specialized court exists to address lawsuits seeking damages for human rights violations. While there are civil remedies for human rights violations through domestic courts, and adverse decisions in human rights cases may be appealed, the majority of human rights cases are brought against nonstate actors. Human rights violations are generally reported to the Independent National Commission on Human Rights, which refers cases to relevant ministries, including the Ministry of

Justice. In some cases individuals and organizations may appeal adverse domestic decisions to regional human rights bodies. While there is an Economic Community of West African States human rights court that Liberians may access, few could afford to do so.

f. Arbitrary or Unlawful Interference with Privacy, Family, Home, or Correspondence

The constitution prohibits such actions, and the government generally respected these prohibitions.

Section 2. Respect for Civil Liberties, Including:

a. Freedom of Speech and Press

The constitution provides for freedom of speech and press, and the government generally respected these rights, although with some limits.

Freedom of Speech and Expression: Individuals could generally criticize the government publicly or privately, but libel, slander, and national security laws placed limits on freedom of speech.

Press and Media Freedoms: According to Reporters without Borders (RSF), media freedom was limited. In August authorities closed two opposition radio stations that broadcast commentary accusing the president of corruption. While the official reason given for the closure was the stations' lack of required permits, other radio stations that lacked permits remained open. Court decisions against journalists involved exorbitant fines, and authorities jailed journalists who did not pay the fines. Self-censorship was widespread; and media often avoided addressing subjects such as the president's family and government corruption.

Violence and Harassment: Law enforcement officers occasionally harassed newspaper and radio station owners because of their political opinions and reporting, especially those that criticized government officials. Government officials harassed and sometimes threatened media members through telephone calls and text messages for political reasons. For example, local press and RSF reported a presidential spokesperson threatened the representative of a journalists' association for calling on the government to reopen radio stations it closed in August. State security forces sometimes arrested journalists for publishing allegedly criminally libelous opinions critical of the government or those with whom the government disagreed. For example, in September plainclothes security officers arrested the editor of the *New Democrat* newspaper and held him for four hours of questioning after he republished an article that accused President Teodoro Obiang of Equatorial Guinea of human rights abuses. The government also used libel and slander laws against print and broadcast media journalists.

Censorship or Content Restrictions: Although generally able to express a wide variety of views, some journalists practiced self-censorship to avoid possible libel charges.

Libel/Slander Laws: There were several reports that libel, slander, and defamation laws constrained the work of journalists and media outlets reporting on high-profile government or other public figures. For example, after reporting on corruption in the award of a high-value road construction contract, a reporter from the *Nation Times* newspaper was arrested and sued for L$200 million ($2.2 million) by the executive awarded the contract. The Press Union of Liberia advocated decriminalizing libel and slander laws to eliminate prison terms for persons unable to pay large fines.

Internet Freedom

The government did not restrict or disrupt access to the internet or censor online content, and there were no reports the government monitored private online communications without appropriate legal authority. According to the International Telecommunication Union, 5.9 percent of the population used the internet during 2015. There were reports of government officials filing civil suits to censor protected speech and intimidate its messengers.

Academic Freedom and Cultural Events

There were no government restrictions on academic freedom or cultural events.

b. Freedom of Peaceful Assembly and Association

The constitution provides for the freedoms of assembly and association, and the government generally respected these rights. Permits are required for public gatherings.

c. Freedom of Religion

See the Department of State's *International Religious Freedom Report* at www.state.gov/religiousfreedomreport/.

d. Freedom of Movement, Internally Displaced Persons, Protection of Refugees, and Stateless Persons

The constitution provides for freedom of internal movement, foreign travel, emigration, and repatriation; the government generally respected these rights.

The government cooperated with the Office of the UN High Commissioner for Refugees (UNHCR), other humanitarian organizations, and donor countries in providing protection and assistance to internally displaced persons, refugees, returning refugees, asylum seekers, stateless persons, and other persons of concern.

In-country Movement: The LNP and Bureau of Immigration and Naturalization officers occasionally subjected travelers to arbitrary searches and petty extortion at official and unofficial checkpoints.

Emigration and Repatriation: In December 2015, following a 16-month suspension due to Ebola concerns, the governments of Cote d'Ivoire and Liberia, with UNHCR assistance, resumed the voluntary repatriation of Ivoirian refugees. Because the land border was still officially closed at that time, the governments established a humanitarian corridor, allowing the overland passage of Ivoirian refugee returnees via UNHCR-organized convoys. In August, Cote d'Ivoire reopened the border, allowing for resumption of regular voluntary repatriation of Ivoirian refugees from the country. Although the rainy season put a temporary damper on the rate of repatriation in the latter part of the year, between December 2015 and August UNHCR and the Liberia Refugee Repatriation and Resettlement Commission assisted the return of more than 19,000 Ivoirian refugees return and expressed an intention to continue to facilitate returns as necessary into 2017. For those Ivoirian refugees wishing to remain in the country, the government worked with UNHCR on developing plans for local integration.

Protection of Refugees

Access to Asylum: The law provides for the granting of asylum or refugee status. The government has an established system for providing protection to refugees and granted refugee status and asylum.

<u>Temporary Protection</u>: The government provided temporary protection to individuals who may not qualify as refugees. The government, with UNHCR and other implementing partners, continued to provide protection to Ivoirian refugees who entered the country after November 2010. As of the end of October, approximately 15,000 Ivoirian refugees remained in the country.

Section 3. Freedom to Participate in the Political Process

The constitution and law provide citizens the ability to choose their government in free and fair periodic elections held by secret ballot and based on universal and equal suffrage.

Elections and Political Participation

<u>Recent Elections</u>: Senate elections were held in 2014. While turnout nationwide at 25 percent was low compared with the 2005 and 2011 general elections, because voting was postponed multiple times due to the Ebola outbreak, it was comparable to turnout for the 2011 constitutional referendum. Only two of 12 incumbent senators retained their seats, and most formal electoral process complaints were resolved through the National Elections Commission or, if appealed, by the Supreme Court. At least two cases were still pending at the Supreme Court. International and national observers declared the elections free, fair, transparent, and credible despite some minor irregularities.

<u>Participation of Women and Minorities</u>: Some observers believed traditional and cultural factors limited women's participation in politics compared to men. Women participated at significantly lower levels than men in voting and as party leaders, civil society activists, and elected officials. According to the Liberia Electoral Access and Participation survey, of registered voters, 43 percent fewer women than men voted in the 2014 Senate elections, and women were 26 percent less likely than men to be registered and vote in the Senate elections. Overall, 25 percent fewer women than men said they were engaged in campaign activities. Although female candidates continued to compete against men at the same proportional levels, the number of women elected to office declined. After the 2011 elections, the percentage of women representatives dropped from 12.5 percent to 9.6 percent and in the Senate from 13.3 percent to 10 percent. During the year there were four women in the 20-member national cabinet, three women in the 30-seat Senate, and nine in the 73-seat House of Representatives. Two female associate justices sat on the five-member Supreme Court. Women

constituted 33 percent of local government officials and 13 percent of senior and deputy ministers.

Section 4. Corruption and Lack of Transparency in Government

The law does not provide explicit criminal penalties for official corruption, although criminal penalties exist for economic sabotage, mismanagement of funds, bribery, and other corruption-related acts. Corruption persisted throughout the government, and the World Bank's most recent Worldwide Governance Indicators reflected that corruption was a serious problem.

Corruption: Some officials engaged in corrupt practices with impunity. Low pay for civil servants, minimal job training, and little judicial accountability exacerbated official corruption and contributed to a culture of impunity. The government dismissed or in some instances suspended officials for alleged corruption and recommended others for prosecution. On May 11, Global Witness released a report that alleged several serving and former senior officials of the government received L$95 million ($1.1 million) in bribes from British firm Sable Mining to obtain an iron ore concession. On May 12, the president appointed a special task force led by Minister of State Without Portfolio Jonathan Koffa to investigate the allegations and recommend prosecution if warranted. On May 25, Speaker of the House of Representatives Tyler and Grand Cape Mount County Senator Varney Sherman were indicted for bribery, criminal conspiracy, economic sabotage, solicitation, and facilitation, based on recommendations by the special task force. In September controversy regarding the indictment led to Tyler's removal from office.

Corruption persisted in the legal system. Some judges accepted bribes to award damages in civil cases. Judges sometimes solicited bribes to try cases, release detainees from prison, or find defendants not guilty in criminal cases. Defense attorneys and prosecutors sometimes suggested defendants pay bribes to secure favorable decisions from judges, prosecutors, and jurors. Corrections officers sometimes demanded payment to escort detainees to trial.

Police corruption was a problem. The LNP investigated reports of police misconduct or corruption, and authorities suspended or dismissed several LNP officers. For example, in February the LNP suspended eight officers from the Criminal Services Division and requested the Ministry of Justice investigate their alleged facilitation of armed robbery. The case was pending with the Ministry of Justice at year's end. In June, LNP authorities dismissed, arrested, and jailed an officer for allegedly taking more than L$1.5 million ($16,725) from 20 individuals as "rent payments" and in September dismissed two officers and suspended seven others for various acts, including extortion and harassment of members of the public.

<u>Financial Disclosure</u>: By regulation senior officials must declare their assets before taking office. There are administrative sanctions for noncompliance.

<u>Public Access to Information</u>: The law provides that the government release upon request information not involving national security issues. Some transparency advocates stated the law did not provide citizens adequate access to verify the proper spending and accounting of government funds.

Section 5. Governmental Attitude Regarding International and Nongovernmental Investigation of Alleged Violations of Human Rights

A number of domestic and international human rights groups operated without government restriction, investigating and publishing their findings on human rights cases. Government officials were generally cooperative and responsive to their views, although sometimes slow to act on requests for assistance on investigations associated with the prosecution of individuals who committed atrocities during the civil war.

<u>Government Human Rights Bodies</u>: The Ministry of Justice Human Rights Protection Division convened monthly coordination meetings that provided a forum for domestic and international human rights NGOs to present matters to the government, including proposed legislation. The UN Office of the High Commissioner for Human Rights (OHCHR) acted as an independent check on the actions of the government in line with its mission to monitor human rights violations in the country. Its work plan included the Palava Hut mechanism, through which community members came together in their towns and villages to discuss grievances and seek reconciliation at the community level. The mechanism was launched in 2012 but remained in the development process with limited geographical reach. During the year the INCHR revamped its operations, including development of a new strategic plan of action, appointment of new staff and human rights monitors, and revitalization of the Palava Hut process.

Section 6. Discrimination, Societal Abuses, and Trafficking in Persons

Women

<u>Rape and Domestic Violence</u>: Rape is illegal, but the government did not enforce the law effectively, and rape remained a serious and pervasive problem. The law's definition of rape does not specifically criminalize spousal rape. Conviction of first-degree rape--defined as rape involving a minor, rape that results in serious injury or disability, or rape committed with the use of a deadly weapon--is punishable by up to life imprisonment. Conviction of second-degree rape, defined as rape committed without the aggravating circumstances enumerated above, is punishable by up to 10 years in prison. Defendants accused of first-degree rape may be denied bail if evidence presented at arraignment meets certain evidentiary standards.

From January to August, the Women's and Children's Protection Section of the LNP received 264 reports of rape, of which 161 were pending investigation and 114 were referred to a specialized sexual violence court (Court E) that has exclusive original jurisdiction over cases of sexual assault, including abuse of minors. Court E's effectiveness was limited by having only one of two authorized judges. A few of the 114 cases referred to Court E were forwarded to criminal court (Court D) for further judicial review. Of 98 cases submitted to the grand jury for prosecution, 89 resulted in indictment. During the year, 22 of 102 prosecuted statutory rape cases resulted in conviction. The true incidence of statutory rape was believed to be much higher than the number of rape cases prosecuted. The Sexual and Gender-based Crimes Unit within the Ministry of Justice continued to improve case management and increased the number of sexual offense indictments. During the year, 290 persons were arrested for sexual offenses and in pretrial detention. Of these, 215 had their initial appearance or first proceeding in front of a judge and 75 remained unprocessed. Of five cases tried, there were two convictions, one mistrial, one acquittal, and one that ended in a hung jury. Prosecutors obtained nine additional convictions through plea bargains.

The Sexual and Gender-based Crimes Unit continued to coordinate with Court E and to collaborate with NGOs and international donors to increase public awareness of sexual and gender-based violence (SGBV) problems; these efforts, according to the government and NGOs, led to increased reporting of rape. Human rights groups claimed the true prevalence of rape was higher than reported.

The government operated two shelters for SGBV victims and victims of trafficking in persons, and established two hotlines for citizens to report SGBV-related crimes. There was also one shelter run by an NGO. The Sexual Pathways Referral program, a combined initiative of the government and NGOs, improved access to medical, psychosocial, legal, and counseling assistance for victims.

The social stigma of rape, especially in rural areas, contributed to the pervasiveness of out-of-court settlements and discouraged formal prosecution of cases. An overtaxed justice system also prevented timely prosecution, although local NGOs pushed for judicial action and sometimes provided lawyers to indigent victims. Due to delays in prosecution, many victims chose to cease cooperating with prosecutors. The government raised awareness of rape through billboards, radio broadcasts, and other outreach campaigns.

Although outlawed, domestic violence remained a widespread problem. The maximum penalty for conviction of domestic violence is six months' imprisonment, but the government did not enforce the law effectively and generally treated cases, if reported, as either simple or aggravated assault.

During the year the Ministry of Gender, Children, and Social Protection organized workshops and seminars to combat domestic violence. Media made some efforts to publicize the problem, and several NGOs continued programs to treat abused women and girls and to increase public awareness of their rights. LNP officers received training on sexual offenses as part of their initial training.

Female Genital Mutilation/Cutting (FGM/C): The law does not specifically prohibit FGM/C, although the government maintained that a 2011 law protecting children against all forms of violence also proscribes FGM/C. The penal code prohibits causing bodily harm with a deadly weapon. No FGM/C perpetrators, however, were prosecuted. It was often performed during initiation into women's secret Sande societies. Less discussed was the use of improper methods for traditional circumcision of boys. While uncommon, young men injured by poorly performed circumcisions may be ostracized by their communities.

In view of the sensitivity of the topic, FGM/C surveys typically eliminate direct reference to FGM/C and instead ask respondents questions regarding initiation into a women's secret society, making it difficult to ascertain actual prevalence rates. According to a 2013 demographic health survey, 50 percent of girls and women ages 15-49 had undergone the procedure. FGM/C was common and traditionally performed on young girls of northern, western, and central ethnic groups, particularly in rural areas and in the poorest households. There were also instances of women age 18 or older being cut, sometimes having married into a practicing community and being shunned by women unless they underwent FGM/C.

According to a 2015 OHCHR report, older women were forcibly initiated into Sande societies as a threat or as punishment for perceived wrongs committed against society members. The percentage of girls and women ages 15 to 49 that underwent FGM/C ranged from 73 percent in the North Central Region to 28 percent in the South Eastern Region.

Government officials routinely engaged traditional leaders to underscore the government's commitment to eliminate FGM/C. The president, minister of internal affairs (as overseer of traditional culture), and the minister of gender, children, and social protection spoke out against the practice, and the Ministry of Justice and Ministry of Gender worked together in an attempt to pass anti-FGM/C legislation. The government routinely decried FGM/C in discussions of violence against women, although there remained some political resistance to passing legislation criminalizing FGM/C because of its association with particular tribes in populous counties.

There was steady movement in prior years toward limiting or prohibiting the practice. The Domestic Violence Bill proposed in January included a provision banning FGM/C on minors without parental consent, or on adults without their consent. In April this provision was removed by the House of Representatives, which prompted movement within the government to propose a stand-alone anti-FGM/C bill.

Sexual Harassment: The law does not specifically prohibit sexual harassment, which remained a major problem, including in schools and places of work. Government billboards and notices in government offices warned against harassment in the workplace.

Reproductive Rights: No laws restrict couples and individuals from deciding the number, spacing, and timing of their children or managing their reproductive health, and individuals have the right to seek and acquire information on reproductive health, free from discrimination, coercion, or violence. Information and assistance on family planning was difficult to obtain, however, particularly in rural areas, where there were few health clinics. The government included family planning counseling and services as key components of its 10-year national health and social welfare plan. The UN Population Division estimated 19.6 percent of girls and women ages 15-49 used a modern method of contraception in 2015. A 2011 government-led survey found that approximately two-thirds of women in similar rural counties said they wanted to use family planning methods. This discrepancy suggested that poverty, lack of government resources, and cultural barriers impeded family planning efforts. The teenage pregnancy rate remained very high.

According to the UN Population Fund's 2015 Trends in Maternal Mortality Report, the country had a maternal mortality rate estimated at 725 per 100,000 live births, and a woman's lifetime risk of maternal death was one in 28. Activities to reduce maternal mortality included additional training of midwives and providing incentives to pregnant women to seek prenatal care and childbirth at a hospital or clinic. Most women delivered outside of health facilities.

Discrimination: By law women may inherit land and property, are entitled to equal pay for equal work, have the right of equal access to education, and may own and manage businesses. Under family law, men retain legal custody of children in divorce cases. Women experienced discrimination in such areas as employment, credit, pay, education, and housing. In rural areas traditional practice or traditional leaders often did not recognize a woman's right to inherit land. Programs to educate traditional leaders on women's rights made some progress, but authorities often did not enforce those rights.

While the law prohibits polygamy, traditional and religious customs permit men to have more than one wife. No specific office exists to enforce the legal rights of women, but the Ministry of Gender, Children, and Social Protection and the Women, Peace, and Security Secretariat--established within the ministry to implement UN Security Council Resolution 1325--generally are responsible for promoting women's rights. The Association of Female Lawyers of Liberia operated a clinic to provide free legal representation to women, with its largest caseload made up of indigent women in child custody actions.

Children

Birth Registration: Children of "Negro" descent born in the country to at least one Liberian parent are citizens. Children born outside the country to a Liberian father are also Liberian citizens. Nevertheless, they may lose that citizenship if they do not reside in Liberia prior to age 21, or if residing abroad they do not take an oath of allegiance before a Liberian consul before age 23. Children born to non-Liberian fathers and Liberian mothers outside of the country do not derive citizenship from the mother. If the father naturalizes as a Liberian citizen prior to a child attaining the age 21, the child may qualify for citizenship. Otherwise, the child must follow normal naturalization procedures. If a child born in the country is not of Negro descent, the child may not acquire citizenship. Non-Negro residents, such as members of the large Lebanese community, may not acquire or transmit citizenship. The law requires parents to register their infants within 14 days of birth, but fewer than 5 percent of births were registered. Even more women than usual did not give birth at health facilities during the Ebola crisis, resulting in thousands of unregistered births. The government acknowledged this problem and took steps to register these children.

Education: The law provides for tuition-free and compulsory education in public schools from the primary (grades one-six) through junior secondary (grades seven-nine) levels, but many schools charged informal fees to pay teachers' salaries and operating costs the government did not fund. These fees prevented many students from attending school. By law fees are required at the senior secondary level (grades 10-12) and, as a practical matter, are essential since the government was unable to fund these schools fully. In both public and private schools, families of students often were required to provide their children's uniforms, books, pencils, paper, and even desks. According to UNICEF only 62 percent of primary school-age children were enrolled in school. The Ministry of Education disagreed, noting that UNICEF data did not take into account the many children enrolled in early childhood education programs. During the year the government began a pilot project with several for-profit education companies to test the feasibility of outsourcing public education. In September some public school teachers went on strike to protest the government's actions, including inadequate pay and job retention reforms.

Girls accounted for fewer than half of all students and graduates in primary and secondary schools, with their proportion decreasing progressively at higher levels. Because parents placed more family responsibilities on daughters, they were more likely to pay school fees for their sons than for their daughters. In addition sexual harassment of girls in schools was commonplace, and adolescent girls were often denied access to school if they became pregnant. Students with disabilities and those in rural counties were most likely to encounter significant barriers to education.

Child Abuse: Widespread child abuse persisted, and reports of sexual violence against children continued. Civil society organizations reported many rapes of children under age 12, and from January to June there were 34 cases of child endangerment reported, of which four cases were being tried, four were pending investigation, and 26 were withdrawn for insufficient evidence or due to lack of cooperation by the complainant. The government engaged in public campaigns to combat child rape.

Early and Forced Marriage: The 2011 National Children's Act sets the marriage age for all persons at 18, while the Domestic Relations Act sets the minimum marriage age at 21 for men and 18 for women. The Equal Rights of the Traditional Marriage Act of 1998 permits a girl to marry at age 16. In partnership with international donors, the government operated a free alternative basic education program for those unable to access formal education that taught life skills such as health, hygiene, birth control, and the merits of delayed marriage. The program, however, operated sporadically. Mass media campaigns were conducted in target communities, especially in rural areas, to educate citizens on the negative consequences of child marriage. Nevertheless, underage marriage remained a problem, especially in rural areas. According to a 2015 UNICEF report, 11 percent of women ages 20 to 24 were married by age 15 and 38 percent were married by age 18.

Female Genital Mutilation/Cutting: See information on girls under 18 in the women's section above.

Sexual Exploitation of Children: The law prohibits the commercial sexual exploitation of children and child pornography, and authorities generally enforced the law, although girls occasionally were exploited in prostitution in exchange for money, food, and school fees. Additionally, sex in exchange for grades was a pervasive problem in secondary schools, with many teachers forcing female students to exchange sexual favors for passing grades. The minimum age for consensual sex is 18. The 2011 National Children's Act sets the marriage age for all persons at 18, while the Domestic Relations Act sets the minimum marriage age at 21 for men and 18 for women. The Equal Rights of the Traditional Marriage Act of 1998 permits a girl to marry at age 16. Statutory rape is a criminal offense that has a maximum sentence if convicted of life imprisonment. During the year the government prosecuted 102 cases of statutory rape. The penalty for conviction of child pornography is up to five years' imprisonment. Orphaned children remained especially susceptible to exploitation, including sex trafficking.

Displaced Children: Despite international and government attempts to reunite children separated from their families during the civil war, some children--a mix of street children, former combatants, and internally displaced persons--continued to live on the streets of Monrovia.

Institutionalized Children: Regulation of orphanages continued to be very weak. Many unofficial orphanages also served as transit points or informal group homes for children, some of whom had living parents who had given them up for possible adoption. Many orphanages lacked adequate sanitation, medical care, and nutrition. They relied primarily on private donations and support from international organizations such as UNICEF and the World Food Program for emergency food and medical and psychological care. Many orphans received no assistance from these institutions. According to the NGO National Concern Youth of Liberia, some groups under the guise of operating an orphanage brought children from rural areas with a promise to provide them with education and then sold the children, often to households in the Monrovia area.

Since the country did not have a facility for their care, juvenile offenders at the MCP routinely were housed in separate cells in adult offender cellblocks. Guidelines existed and steps occasionally were taken to divert juveniles from the formal criminal justice system and place them in a variety of safe homes and "kinship" care situations.

International Child Abductions: The country is not a party to the 1980 Hague Convention on the Civil Aspects of International Child Abduction. See the Department of State's *Annual Report on International Parental Child Abduction* at travel.state.gov/content/childabduction/en/legal/compliance.html.

Anti-Semitism

There was a small Jewish community, and there were no reports of anti-Semitic acts.

Trafficking in Persons

See the Department of State's *Trafficking in Persons Report* at www.state.gov/j/tip/rls/tiprpt/.

Persons with Disabilities

Although it is illegal to discriminate against persons with physical and mental disabilities, such persons did not enjoy equal access to government services and found very limited employment prospects. The constitution prohibits discrimination against persons with physical, sensory, intellectual, or mental disabilities in employment and provides for access to health care, the judicial system, and other state services, but these provisions were not always enforced. Government buildings were not easily accessible to persons with mobility disabilities, and sign language interpretation was not provided for deaf persons in criminal proceedings or in the provision of state services. There is a legal prohibition against discrimination on such grounds in accessing air travel or other transportation.

Few children with disabilities had access to education. Public educational institutions discriminated against students with disabilities, arguing resources and equipment were insufficient to accommodate them. During the year the legislature passed a law prohibiting school administrators from discriminating against students with disabilities or denying them admission to schools based on inadequate school resources.

Many citizens had permanent disabilities resulting from the civil war. Persons with disabilities faced societal exclusion, particularly in rural areas. The government included persons with disabilities in its 2012 Vision 2030 National Development Strategy and related panel discussions that continued during the year. In August a Monrovia church taught LNP, Drug Enforcement Agency, and Bureau of Immigration and Naturalization officers basic sign language to facilitate communication with deaf citizens and suspects.

Students with more significant disabilities are exempt from compulsory education but may attend school subject to constraints on accommodating them. In reality few such students were able to attend either private or public schools. There were a small number of private schools located in urban areas specialized in education for persons with disabilities, but these schools had limited resources.

The right of persons with disabilities to vote and otherwise participate in civic affairs is legally protected and generally respected. The inaccessibility of buildings posed problems for persons with limited mobility wishing to exercise these rights. The Ministry of Gender, Children, and Social Protection is the government agency responsible for protecting the rights of persons with disabilities and implementing measures designed to improve respect for their rights.

National/Racial/Ethnic Minorities

Although the law prohibits ethnic discrimination, racial discrimination is enshrined in the constitution, which restricts citizenship and land ownership to those of "Negro descent." While persons of Lebanese and Asian descent who were born or who have lived most of their lives in the country may not by law attain citizenship or own land, there were some exceptions.

Indigenous People

The law recognizes 16 indigenous ethnic groups; each speaks a distinct primary language and is concentrated regionally. Long-standing disputes regarding land and other resources among ethnic groups continued to contribute to social and political tensions.

Acts of Violence, Discrimination, and Other Abuses Based on Sexual Orientation and Gender Identity

The law prohibits consensual same-sex sexual activity, and the culture is strongly opposed to homosexuality. "Voluntary sodomy" is a misdemeanor with a penalty for conviction of up to one year's imprisonment. LGBTI activists reported that LGBTI persons faced difficulty in obtaining redress for crimes committed against them, including at police stations, because those accused of criminal acts used the victim's LGBTI status as a defense. For example, an individual who was beaten sought police assistance but rather than investigate the victim's allegation, police arrested the victim because the alleged perpetrator accused him of being gay. In October an LGBTI advocacy group reported several individuals were arrested and accused of sodomy; one of them was arrested after he reported being robbed to police.

The law prohibits same-sex couples, regardless of citizenship, from adopting children. LGBTI persons were cautious about revealing their sexual orientation or gender identities. A few civil society groups promoted the rights of LGBTI individuals, but most groups maintained a very low profile due to fear of mistreatment. Additionally, societal stigma and fear of official reprisal prevented some victims from reporting violence or discrimination based on sexual orientation or gender identity. For example, an LGBTI advocacy group reported instances of women being raped to "correct" their sexual orientation, but women rarely reported rapes to the police due to fear and social stigma surrounding both sexual orientation and rape.

LGBTI individuals faced discrimination in accessing housing, health care, employment, and education. For example, in October an individual working for the Ministry of Health was "outed" by a coworker who repeatedly derided him at work, and the ministry failed to order an end to the harassment or otherwise respond. LGBTI advocacy groups also reported children quitting school due to bullying related to sexual identity and orientation.

There were press and civil society reports of harassment of persons perceived to be LGBTI, with some newspapers targeting the LGBTI community. For example, in June *The Inquirer* newspaper published a cartoon and sponsored an essay contest on whether FGM/C or homosexuality was worse for society. Some politicians, to garner support, made public statements against the rights of the LGBTI community.

On the other hand, the Ministry of Health created a coordinator to assist minority groups--including LGBTI persons--in obtaining access to health care and police assistance. A civil society group provided human rights training on LGBTI issues to communities, including to local police and others promoted LGBTI access to judicial and health services by networking with and training lawyers. An LGBTI rights advocacy group provided human rights training to female police and immigration officers.

HIV and AIDS Social Stigma

The most recent demographic and health survey in 2013 found no measurable improvement since 2007 in popular attitudes, which remained broadly discriminatory toward those with HIV. HIV-related social stigma and discrimination discouraged persons from testing for their HIV status, thus limiting HIV prevention and treatment services. Children orphaned because of AIDS faced similar social stigma.

Government ministries developed, adopted, and implemented several strategic plans to combat social stigma and discrimination based on HIV status. The Ministry of Labor continued to promote a supportive environment for persons with HIV. The Ministry of Education continued implementation of its strategic plan to destigmatize and safeguard HIV-positive persons against discrimination in its recruitment, employment, admission, and termination processes. The law prohibits "discrimination and vilification on the basis of actual and perceived HIV status" in the workplace, school, and health facilities, with conviction of offenses punishable by a fine of no less than L$1,000 ($11).

Other Societal Violence or Discrimination

Mob violence and vigilantism, due in part to the public's lack of confidence in police and the judicial system, resulted in deaths and injuries. For example, in September the threat of intertribal violence in Voinjama forced residents to hide or flee from an angry mob of ethnic Mandingos after police refused to release a Lorma man accused of ritually killing a Mandingo man. According to multiple reports, the Mandingo mob threatened to storm the police station and seize the Lorma man. The mob did not act on the threat.

There were also reports of increased stigmatization of Ebola survivors and their families and health-care workers who had worked in Ebola treatment facilities. According to the Ebola Survivors Network, survivors and their families confronted discrimination from landlords, neighbors, health-care providers, and employers.

There were reports of killings in which body parts were removed from the victim, a practice possibly related to ritual killings. On March 2, the Second Judicial Circuit Court in Grand Bassa County convicted three men of murdering Nimley Tarr in 2014 for ritualistic purposes and sentenced them to death by hanging. According to the court record, the convicted men lured and murdered Tarr for his body parts. Ritual killings were reportedly on the increase during the year, but it was difficult to ascertain exact numbers since ritual killings were often attributed to homicide, accidents, or suicide.

Section 7. Worker Rights

a. Freedom of Association and the Right to Collective Bargaining

The law provides workers, except public servants and employees of state-owned enterprises, the right to freely form or join independent unions of their choice without prior authorization or excessive requirements. It allows unions to conduct their activities without interference by employers. The law provides that labor organizations and associations have the right to draw up their constitutions and rules with regard to electing their representatives, organizing their activities, and formulating their programs. The law provides for the right of workers to bargain collectively. The law also provides for the right of workers to conduct legal strikes. Workers have the right to strike, provided they notify the Ministry of Labor of the intent to strike. The law also prohibits antiunion discrimination. The law requires reinstatement of workers fired for union activity. The law prohibits unions from engaging in partisan political activity and prohibits agricultural workers from joining industrial workers' organizations.

While the law prohibits antiunion discrimination and provides for reinstatement for workers dismissed for union activity, it allows for dismissal without cause if the company provides the mandated severance package. It also does not prohibit retaliation against strikers whose strikes comply with the law. Section 41.3(d) of the Decent Work Act of 2015 states, "An employer may not institute civil legal proceedings against a person who participates in a strike or lockout in compliance with this chapter, unless those proceedings concern an act that constitutes defamation or a criminal offense, or unless the proceedings arise from an employee being dismissed for a valid reason."

In general the government effectively enforced applicable laws, and workers exercised their rights. Employees enjoy freedom of association, and they have the right to establish and become members of organizations of their own choosing without previous authorization or coercion. The law, however, does not provide adequate protection, since it imposes inadequate sanctions and depends on whether property damage has occurred and is measurable. Penalties were inadequate to deter violations. Administrative and judicial procedures were subject to lengthy delays or appeals and to outside interference.

Government and employers usually respected the freedom of association and collective bargaining. Union power continued to increase during the year through increased membership at plantations; however, only a small fraction of the workforce was employed in the formal sector, and more than 80 percent of workers did not enjoy any formal legal labor protections. The lack of formal protections caused tensions in particular in the iron ore and rubber industries, where companies drastically reduced operations due to the global downturn in demand for these commodities. Labor unions called on the legislature to pass laws that would improve work conditions across the country and succeeded with the publication of the Decent Work Act into law. Although issues of wages remained critical in agriculture sector bargaining, unions also focused on other issues, including better housing, health, and schools. Unions were independent of the government and political parties. There were no reports of discrimination or employer retaliation against strikers during the year.

b. Prohibition of Forced or Compulsory Labor

The law prohibits all forms of forced or compulsory labor, but the government did not effectively enforce such laws. Resources, inspections, and remediation were inadequate. The law prescribes a minimum sentence of one year's imprisonment for the trafficking of adults but does not prescribe a maximum sentence; these penalties were neither sufficiently stringent nor commensurate with the penalties prescribed for other serious offenses, such as rape.

Forced labor occurred. Families living in the interior sometimes sent young women and children to stay with relatives in Monrovia or other cities with the promise that the relatives would assist the women and children to pursue educational or other opportunities. In some instances these women and children were forced to work as street vendors, domestic servants, or beggars. While there are no official records regarding labor, young women and children also were subject to forced labor on rubber plantations and in gold mines, rock-crushing quarries, and alluvial diamond mines. While the government worked to decrease incidence, in some communities child labor was considered part of normal life, as poverty surpassed any legal considerations. Forced labor continued despite efforts by NGOs and other organizations to eliminate the practice.

When victims were identified, the Women and Children Protection Section of the LNP, along with NGOs, worked to reunite victims with their families in the interior or referred them to safe homes. Child labor continued to be addressed as a child endangerment problem; consequently, no reliable figures were available on the number of children removed from forced labor. The government took a few steps to prevent or eliminate forced labor, including periodic labor inspections to enforce the Children's Law and the Decent Work Act and cooperation with international donors on projects to eliminate child labor in the rubber sector.

See the Department of State's *Trafficking in Persons Report* at www.state.gov/j/tip/rls/tiprpt/.

c. Prohibition of Child Labor and Minimum Age for Employment

Under the Decent Work Act, full-time employment for children under the age of 15 is prohibited. Children above age 13 but under age 15 may be employed to perform "light work" for a maximum of two hours per day and not more than 14 hours per week. "Light work" is defined as work that does not prejudice the child's attendance at school or their capacity to benefit from instruction and is not likely to be harmful to a child's health or safety and moral or material welfare or development. There is an exception to the law for artistic performances, and the law leaves the determination of times of day a child may work open for later regulation by the minister of labor. Under the act children age 15 and under are not allowed to work more than seven hours a day, or more than 42 hours in a week. There are mandatory rest periods of one hour, and the child may not work more than four hours consecutively. The law also prohibits the employment of children under age 16 during school hours, unless the employer keeps a registry of the child's school certificate to illustrate the child attended school regularly and can demonstrate the child was able to read and write simple sentences. The law prohibits the employment of apprentices under age 16. The compulsory education requirement extends through grade nine or until age 15.

Although the National Children's Act supplements other laws by prohibiting any work hazardous to a child's health and educational, emotional, or physical development, it does not define the types of hazardous work, a deficiency in part corrected by passage of the Decent Work Act. According to the act, hazardous work that is prohibited for children includes: work that exposes children to physical, psychological, or sexual abuse; work underground, under water, at dangerous heights, or in confined spaces; work with dangerous machinery, equipment, and tools, or that involves the manual handling or transport of heavy loads; work in an unhealthy environment that may, for example, expose children to hazardous substances, agents, or processes, or to temperatures, noise levels, or vibrations damaging to their health; or work under particularly difficult conditions such as long hours or during the night, or work where the child is unreasonably confined to the premises of the employer. Terms under this provision of the law are poorly defined, which hinders the ability of labor inspectors and police officers to enforce child labor laws effectively.

According to the law, "a parent, caregiver, guardian, or relative who engages in any act or connives with any other person to subject a child to sexual molestation, prohibited child labor, or such other act, that places the well-being of a child at risk is guilty of a second-degree felony."

The Child Labor Commission is responsible for enforcing child labor laws and policies, although it did not do so effectively, in part due to inadequate staff and funding. As a result, while inspectors were trained, none was specifically assigned to monitor and address child labor. The labor commission coordinated efforts to provide scholarships for children to enroll in school. The government charged the Ministry of Labor's Child Labor Secretariat, the Ministry of Justice's Human Rights Division, the Ministry of Gender, Children and Social Protection's Human Rights Division, the Ministry of Health's Department of Social Welfare, and the LNP's Women's and Children's Protection Section with investigating and referring for prosecution allegations of child labor; however, inspections and remediation were inadequate.

The law penalizes employers that violate the minimum age provision of child labor laws with a fine of L$100 ($1.12) and imprisonment until the fine is paid. The law also penalizes parents or guardians who violate this minimum age provision with a minimum fine of L$15 ($0.17) but not more than L$25 ($0.28) and imprisonment until such fine is paid. These penalties were insufficient to deter violations. In October members of the LNP briefly detained children found selling goods in the streets around Monrovia. The children were released after their parents and guardians paid fines at the police depots where they were held. The Ministry of Labor was not involved in the operation.

Child labor was widespread in almost every economic sector. In urban areas children assisted their parents as vendors in markets or hawked goods on the streets. There were reports that children tapped rubber on smaller plantations and private farms. There were also reports that children worked in conditions likely to harm their health and safety, such as rock crushing or work that required carrying heavy loads. Some children were engaged in hazardous labor in alluvial diamond and gold mining as well as in the agriculture sector.

The government held regularly scheduled sensitization and training activities, often funded by international donors, and the Division of Child Labor worked during the year with the Child Labor Commission to develop a national action plan to address child labor. Passage of the Decent Work Act and its provisions on child labor were a significant step forward, and the National Action Plan to Address Child Labor was with the International Labor Organization and UNICEF for validation.

International NGOs worked to eliminate the worst forms of child labor by withdrawing children from hazardous work and putting at-risk children in school. Other local and international NGOs worked to raise awareness of the worst forms of child labor.

See the Department of Labor's *Findings on the Worst Forms of Child Labor* at www.dol.gov/ilab/reports/child-labor/findings/.

d. Discrimination with Respect to Employment and Occupation

A constitutional provision (Article 18) prohibits discrimination with respect to equal opportunity for work and employment regardless of sex, creed, religion, ethnic background, place of origin, or political affiliation, and calls for equal pay for equal work. The government in general did not effectively enforce the law. The law does not prohibit discrimination in the workplace regarding language, race, color, age, disability, HIV-positive status or having other communicable diseases, sexual orientation, or gender identity.

Discrimination in employment and occupation occurred with respect to gender, disability, HIV-positive status, sexual orientation, and gender identity. Apart from facing economic discrimination based on cultural traditions, women also experienced discrimination in employment. Although Article 18 of the constitution prohibits discrimination in employment and provides for equal pay for equal work, the law does not explicitly prohibit discrimination in hiring based on gender, and women experienced economic discrimination based on cultural traditions resisting their employment outside the home in rural areas. The Ministry of Gender and related government programs and partnerships with NGOs promoted women's participation in the economic sector, including through initiatives such as workshops on networking, entrepreneurial skills, and microcredit lending. Disabled individuals faced hiring discrimination, as well as difficulty with workplace access and accommodation (see section 6, Persons with Disabilities).

e. Acceptable Conditions of Work

The Decent Work Act requires a minimum wage of L$43 ($0.48) per hour (increased from $0.17 prior to the Decent Work Act's passage), or L$350 ($3.90) per day (not exceeding eight hours per day), excluding benefits, for unskilled laborers. This applies to the informal economic sector including domestic, agricultural, and casual workers. The minimum wage for the formal economic sector is L$69 ($0.77) per hour, or L$550 ($6.13) per day (not exceeding eight hours per day), excluding benefits. Although the law does fix a minimum wage for agricultural workers, it allows that they be paid at the rate agreed in the collective bargaining agreement between workers' unions and management, excluding benefits (provided the amounts agreed to should not be less than the legally stipulated minimums). Although the law stipulates the minimum rates, skilled labor has no minimum fixed wage as wages differ across professions, industries and sectors, and the average salary for civil servants was L$10,000-L$12,000 ($112-$134) per month.

Many families paid minimum-wage incomes were also engaged in subsistence farming, small-scale marketing, and begging. The national poverty line is L$125 ($1.39) per day. According to the United Nations, 64 percent of citizens lived below the poverty line.

The law provides for a 48-hour, six-day regular workweek with a 30-minute rest period for every five hours of work. The six-day workweek may be extended to 56 hours for service occupations and 72 hours for miners. The law provides for pay for overtime and prohibits excessive compulsory overtime.

The law provides for paid leave, severance benefits, and occupational health and safety standards; the standards are current and appropriate for the intended industries. Workers cannot remove themselves from situations that endanger health or safety without jeopardy to their employment, however, and authorities did not effectively protect employees in this situation. Penalties were not sufficient to deter violations.

The Ministry of Labor's Labor Inspection Department enforced government-established health and safety standards. These standards were not enforced in all sectors, including the informal economy. Every county has a labor commissioner, and depending on the county one to two labor inspectors. These inspectors are responsible only for monitoring labor in the formal sector, however, and there is no system for monitoring the informal sector. The ministry had approximately 25 inspectors throughout the country to investigate allegations of labor violations. The number of inspectors was not sufficient to enforce compliance. The department assigned these inspectors to assist county labor commissioners in all counties, and they mainly monitored the formal sector. The department was grossly understaffed at the county level, and inspectors frequently lacked working vehicles. Although a few counties had four-wheel drive vehicles, most had only a motorbike. In instances of breach of standards, fines were imposed on violators, but often these were an insufficient deterrent. Delinquent violators were not regularly sent to the labor court. Enforcement of standards and inspection findings was not always consistent.

Most citizens were unable to find work in the formal sector and therefore did not benefit from any of the formal labor laws and protections. The vast majority (estimated at 85 percent) had no other option than to work in the (largely unregulated) informal sector, where they faced widely varying and often harsh working conditions. Informal workers included rock crushers, artisanal miners, agricultural workers, street sellers, domestic workers, and others. In the diamond and gold mines, in addition to physical danger and poor working conditions, the industry is unregulated, leaving minors vulnerable to exploitive brokers, dealers, and intermediaries.

www.ingramcontent.com/pod-product-compliance
Lightning Source LLC
Chambersburg PA
CBHW081256250726
48654CB00012B/1629